ISBN 978-0-331-88378-7
PIBN 11039656

1 MONTH OF
FREE
READING

at

www.ForgottenBooks.com

By purchasing this book you are eligible for one month membership to ForgottenBooks.com, giving you unlimited access to our entire collection of over 1,000,000 titles via our web site and mobile apps.

To claim your free month visit:

www.forgottenbooks.com/free1039656

English
Français
Deutsche
Italiano
Español
Português

www.forgottenbooks.com

Mythology Photography **Fiction**
Fishing Christianity **Art** Cooking
Essays Buddhism Freemasonry
Medicine **Biology** Music **Ancient
Egypt** Evolution Carpentry Physics
Dance Geology **Mathematics** Fitness
Shakespeare **Folklore** Yoga Marketing
Confidence Immortality Biographies
Poetry **Psychology** Witchcraft
Electronics Chemistry History **Law**
Accounting **Philosophy** Anthropology
Alchemy Drama Quantum Mechanics
Atheism Sexual Health **Ancient History**
Entrepreneurship Languages Sport
Paleontology Needlework Islam
Metaphysics Investment Archaeology
Parenting Statistics Criminology
Motivational

POLITICAL ECONOMY CLUB,

FOUNDED IN LONDON, 1821.

NAMES OF MEMBERS

1821—1872:—

RULES OF THE CLUB:—

AND

LIST OF QUESTIONS DISCUSSED,

1860—1872:

VOLUME II.

IN CONTINUATION OF VOLUME I. PUBLISHED IN 1860,
CONTAINING THE QUESTIONS DISCUSSED, 1833–60.

LONDON:

PRINTED FOR THE CLUB.

1872.

THE Political Economy Club was founded in London in the year 1821, chiefly by the exertions of the late Thomas Tooke, F.R.S.

From the date of foundation to the year 1850, the meetings of the Club were held at the Freemason's Tavern, Great Queen Street. From 1850 to 1861, they were held at the Thatched House Tavern, St. James's Street; from 1861 to 1867, at the St. James's, 71, Quadrant, Regent Street; and since that time, at Willis's Rooms, King Street, St. James's Square.

The Club usually meets on the first Friday in each month from December to July, both inclusive, but omitting January, in which month there is no meeting.

CONTENTS.

PART I.

LIST OF MEMBERS, DECEMBER 1872.

Elected.	*Name.*
O.M. 1821	GEORGE W. NORMAN.
April 1834	EDWIN CHADWICK, C.B.
,, 1835	WILLIAM JOHN BLAKE, F.R.S.
,, ,,	HIS EXCELLENCY M. VAN DE WEYER.
,, 1836	JOHN STUART MILL.
,, 1837	GEORGE J. GRAHAM.
Feb. 1847	HERMAN MERIVALE, C.B.
Mar. ,,	LORD BELPER.
,, ,,	WILLIAM T. THORNTON.

NOTE.—O.M. signifies Original Member, 1821.

Elected.	Name.
Mar. 1850	JOHN GELLIBRAND HUBBARD.
Dec. 1852	WILLIAM NEWMARCH, F.R.S.
Mar. 1855	Sir GEORGE W. BRAMWELL.
April ,,	THOMSON HANKEY.
Mar. 1858	CHARLES MORRISON.
May ,,	JOHN ALEXANDER HANKEY.
,, 1859	Sir JOHN MACPHERSON MACLEOD.
Feb. 1860	HENRY THRING.
June 1862	Hon. E. F. LEVESON GOWER.
Dec. 1863	Sir EDWARD W. WATKIN.
May 1864	WALTER BAGEHOT.
Dec. ,,	T. H. FARRER.
Feb. 1865	THOMAS HARE.
June ,,	JACOB WALEY.

Elected.	Name.
May 1866	EARL DUFFERIN.
Feb. 1867	LORD FREDERICK CAVENDISH, M.P.
Mar. ,,	Sir JOHN LUBBOCK, BART., M.P.
April ,,	W. R. GREG.
,, 1869	LEONARD H. COURTNEY.
,, ,,	Sir ROBERT R. TORRENS, M.P.
May ,,	Sir CHARLES W. DILKE, BART., M.P.
Feb. 1870	Sir LOUIS MALLET, C.B.
Mar. 1871	GEORGE J. SHAW LEFEVRE, M.P.
,, 1872	JOHN MORLEY.

Under the Rule that Members of the Club becoming Cabinet Ministers thereupon become Honorary Members,

THE FOLLOWING ARE HONORARY MEMBERS.

Became Hon. Mem.	*Name.*	*Elected Member.*
1836	EARL GREY	1833
1851	EARL GRANVILLE	*Feb.* 1850
July 1859	Rt. Hon. C. P. VILLIERS, M.P.	*Mar.* 1847
June 1865	Rt.Hon.W.E.GLADSTONE,M.P.	*June* 1865
April 1866	Rt. Hon. G. J. GÖSCHEN, M.P.	*Mar.* ,,
Feb. 1869	EARL OF KIMBERLEY	*May* 1857
Feb. ,,	Rt. Hon. ROBERT LOWE, M.P.	*Mar.* 1853
Dec. 1870	Rt.Hon.W. E. FORSTER, M.P.	*Apr.* 1869

LORD OVERSTONE *is also an Honorary Member.*

By a Resolution of the Club dated 6th March, 1862, Six Honorary Members may be elected from the Incumbents for the time being of the following *Professorships of Political Economy*, viz.:—

POLITICAL ECONOMY IN *University of Oxford.*

POLITICAL ECONOMY IN *University of Cambridge.*

POLITICAL ECONOMY IN *University College, London.*

ECONOMIC SCIENCE AND STATISTICS, *King's College, London.*—TOOKE FOUNDATION.

POLITICAL ECONOMY, *Trinity College, Dublin.*—WHATELY FOUNDATION.

POLITICAL ECONOMY, *Queen's College, Belfast.*

POLITICAL ECONOMY, *Queen's College, Cork.*

POLITICAL ECONOMY, *Queen's College, Galway.*

The present Honorary Members under this arrangement are :—

BONAMY PRICE, *Oxford.*

HENRY FAWCETT, M.P., *Cambridge.*

J. E. T. ROGERS, *King's College, London.*

T. E. C. LESLIE, *Queen's College, Belfast.*

J. C. CAIRNES, *Queen's College, Galway.*

―――――――――

The Members of the Committee of the Club are MR. NEWMARCH *(Treasurer), and* MR. WALEY *(Hon. Secretary).*

PART II.

Name.	Died.	Resigned.
1821. *Original Members.*		
GEORGE BASEVI,	——	*Jan.* 1831
G. BROWN,	*May* 1829	——
I. CAZENOVE,	——	*Jan.* 1831
JOHN WELSFORD COWELL,	*Feb.* 1869	——
WILLIAM KEITH DOUGLAS,	——	*Dec.* 1822
HENRY ENTWISTLE,	1838	——
GEORGE GROTE,	——	*Dec.* 1831
SWINTON C. HOLLAND,	*Jan.* 1828	——
SIR G. G. DE H. LARPENT, *Bt*	——	*Feb.* 1849
SIR J. G. S. LEFEVRE, K.C.B.	——	*Feb.* 1831

Name.	Died.	Resigned.
1821. *Original Members.*		
GEORGE LYALL, M.P.,	——	*Dec.* 1849
W. L. MABERLY,	——	*May* 1829
ZACHARY MACAULAY,	——	*Dec.* 1831
J. L. MALLET,	——	*Feb.* 1836
REV. ROBERT MALTHUS,	*eb.* 1835	——
JAMES MILL,	*Dec.* 1835	——
F. MITCHELL,	——	*Dec.* 1822
ROBERT MUSHET,	——	*Feb.* 1828
GEORGE WARDE NORMAN,		
SIR HENRY PARNELL, M.P., (*Lord Congleton,* 1839).	1841	——
ALEXANDER PREVOST,	——	*Mar.* 1829
CHARLES PRINSEP,	——	*April* 1824
DAVID RICARDO, M.P.,	*Sept.* 1823	——
EDWARD SIMSON,	——	*Dec.* 1824
R. SIMPSON,	*May* 1828	——

	Name.	Died.	Resigned

1821.   *Original Members.*

	JOHN ABEL SMITH, M.P.,	——	*Jan.* 185
	THOMAS TOOKE, F.R.S.,	*Feb.* 1858	——
	COLONEL ROBERT TORRENS,	——	*Mar.* 185
	HENRY WARBURTON, M.P.,	*Sept.* 1858	——

Elected 1821.

	WALTER COULSON,	*Dec.* 1860	

1823.

Feb.	NASSAU WILLIAM SENIOR,	*July* 1864	——
June	LORD ALTHORP,	1845	——
	(Earl Spencer, 1834.)		

1824.

Feb.	MOSES RICARDO,	——	184
May	WILLIAM W. WHITMORE, M.P.,	*Sept.* 1857	——

1825.

Jan.	J. S. RAVENSHAW,	——	*Jan.* 182

1828.

Feb.	JAMES PENNINGTON,	——	*July* 185
Mar.	WILLIAM BINGHAM BARING M.P.	*April* 1864	——
	(Lord Ashburton, 1848.)		
,,	CHARLES P. THOMSON, M.P.,	1841	——
	(Hon. Member, 1835. Lord Sydenham, 1840.)		

	Name.	Died.	Resigned.
	Elected 1828.		
June	H. St. John Mildmay,	——	*Feb.* 1832
	1829.		
,,	James R. McCulloch,	——	1846
Dec.	John Horsley Palmer,	——	*Dec.* 1846
,,	Rt. Hon. Sir R. W. Horton,	——	*June* 1831
	1831.		
Jan.	William Blake,	*Nov.* 1852	——
Mar.	Samuel Jones Loyd,		
	(*Lord Overstone,* 1850. *Hon. Member,* 1872.)		
June	Hyde Villiers,	——	*Dec.* 1832
Dec.	Colonel Perronet Thompson,	——	*Mar.* 1835
	1832.		
Jan.	Rt. Hon. Thomas S. Rice, M.P.,	1866	——
	(*Hon. Member,* 1834. *Lord Monteagle,* 1839.)		
,,	Sir John Romilly,	——	*June* 1872
	(*Lord Romilly,* 1865.)		
Feb.	Charles Hay Cameron,	——	*Dec.* 1859
	1833.		
,,	George Villiers,	——	*Feb.* 1834
	(*Hon. Member. Lord Clarendon,* 1839.)		
	1834.		
,,	James Deacon Hume,	*Feb.* 1841	——

Name.	Died.	Resigned.

Elected 1834.

	Name	Died	Resigned
Mar.	JAMES MORRISON,	*Oct.* 1857	——
April	EDWIN CHADWICK, C.B.,		

1835.

,,	SYLVAIN VAN DE WEYER,		
,,	CHARLES BULLER, M.P.,	*Dec.* 1848	——
,,	WILLIAM JOHN BLAKE,		

1836.

,,	JOHN LOUIS PREVOST,	*Sept.* 1852	——
,,	JOHN STUART MILL,		
,,	MARQUIS OF LANSDOWNE,	1866	——
April	EARL OF KERRY,	1836	——
,,	Rt. Hon. HOLT. MACKENZIE,	——	*Jan.* 1867
,,	G. J. GRAHAM,		

1837.

May	SIR WILLIAM CLAY, BT., M.P.,	*Mar.* 1869	——

1840.

April	SAMPSON RICARDO, M.P.,	*June* 1863	——

1841.

Mar.	GEORGE ROBERT PORTER,	*Aug.* 1852	——

Name.	Died.	R(

Elected 1841.

May	REV. SIDNEY SMITH,	——	*Feb*

1843.

| *Feb.* | THOMAS VARDON, | —— | *Fel* |
| *Mar.* | COUNT POLLON, | 1846 | - |

1847.

Feb.	HERMAN MERIVALE, C.B.,		
Mar.	EDWARD STRUTT, M.P., (*Lord Belper*, 1856).		
,,	Rt. Hon. C. P. VILLIERS, M.P.,		
,,	Rt. Hon. E. P. BOUVERIE, M.P.,	——	*De(*
,,	WILLIAM T. THORNTON,		
.,	JOHN LEWIS RICARDO, M.P.,	——	*Apr*
Mar.	SIR BENJAMIN HAWES, K.C.B.,	——	*Dec.*

1850.

| *Feb.* | EARL GRANVILLE, | | |
| *Mar.* | JOHN GELLIBRAND HUBBARD, M.P., | | |

1851.

| *May* | LORD WODEHOUSE,
(*Hon Member. Earl of Kimberley*, 1866.) | | |

	Name.	Died.	Resigned.

Elected 1852.

Dec.	WILLIAM NEWMARCH, F.R.S.,		

1853.

Mar.	Rt. Hon. ROBERT LOWE, M.P.,		
,,	KIRKMAN D. HODGSON, M.P.,	——	*Mar.* 1869

1855.

,,	SIR GEORGE W. W. BRAMWELL,		
Apr.	THOMSON HANKEY, M.P.,		

1857.

Feb.	Rt. Hon. SIR G. C. LEWIS, M.P.,	1863	——
,,	WM. ARTHUR WILKINSON,	*May* 1865	——

1858.

,,	SIR ROWLAND HILL, K.C.B.,	——	*Dec.* 1872
Mar.	CHARLES MORRISON,		
May	JOHN ALEXANDER HANKEY,		
June	HENRY THOMAS BUCKLE,	——	*Jan.* 1860

1859.

May	Sir JOHN MACPHERSON MACLEOD,		

Name.	Died.	F

Elected 1860.

Feb.	HENRY THRING,		
June	GEORGE M. W. PEACOCKE, M.P.,	——	*Fe*

1861.

Mar.	HENRY FAWCETT, M.P.,		
June	SIR STAFFORD NORTHCOTE, Bt.,	——	*De*

1862.

	Hon. E. F. LEVESON GOWER, M.P.,		

1863.

Feb.	J. FITZJAMES STEPHEN, Q.C.,	——	*De*
Dec.	SIR EDWARD W. WATKIN,		

1864.

May	WALTER BAGEHOT,		
Dec.	T. H. FARRER,		

1865.

Feb.	THOMAS HARE,		
Mar.	G. J. GÖSCHEN,		
June	JACOB WALEY,		

1866.

May	LORD DUFFERIN,		

D

	Name.	*Died.*	F

Elected 1867.

Feb.   LORD FREDERICK CAVENDISH, M.P.,

Mar.   SIR JOHN LUBBOCK, Bt.,

April   W. R. GREG,

1869.

Mar.   SIR ROBERT R. TORRENS, M.P.,

Rt. Hon. W. E. FORSTER, M.P.,

April   LEONARD H. COURTNEY,

May   SIR CHAS. W. DILKE, Bt., M.P.,

1870.

Feb.   SIR LOUIS MALLET, C.B.,

1871.

Mar.   GEORGE J. SHAW LEFEVRE, M.P.,

1872.

JOHN MORLEY,

PART III.

RULES OF THE CLUB.

1. The number of the Members of the Club is limited to Thirty-five.

2. Foreigners usually resident out of the United Kingdom are eligible as Honorary Members.

3. The Club may elect not more than six Honorary Members from the Incumbents, for the time being, of the following Professorships of Political Economy, viz.:—POLITICAL ECONOMY, in University of Oxford; POLITICAL ECONOMY, in University of Cambridge; POLITICAL ECONOMY, in University Coll., London; ECONOMIC SCIENCE AND STATISTICS, King's Coll., London, TOOKE foundation; POLITICAL ECONOMY, Trinity Coll.,

Dublin, WHATELY foundation; POLITICAL ECONOMY, Queen's Coll., Belfast; POLITICAL ECONOMY, Queen's Coll., Cork; POLITICAL ECONOMY, Queen's Coll., Galway.

4. The name of a Candidate shall be communicated to the Club, together with that of the members who propose him, one Meeting at least before the Election.

5. New Members should be chosen by ballot, the assent of two-thirds of the Members present being required to constitute a member.

6. In case of more Candidates than vacancies, the order in which the Candidates shall be proposed shall be determined by a previous Ballot.

7. Any Member intending to reside abroad for a year or more may vacate his seat, upon condition, if he require it, of being re-elected without ballot, on the first vacancy after his return.

8. The Club shall meet on the *first Friday* in

December, and on the first Friday in every month from February to July inclusive, or on such other days as shall be determined by a vote of the Club. The Subscription to be Five Guineas per annum for each Member, which is to be paid to the Treasurer, or to the Banker appointed by him, on the first of January in each year.

9. Any Four Members (not Honorary) may introduce a stranger, on giving, on or before the day next before the day of Meeting, a written notice of their intention; such notice to contain the name of the stranger and the names of the four introducers. The name of no person to be used who has not verbally, or by writing, assented to the particular introduction in question. Any Member, Honorary or not, may introduce a stranger without such notice, on paying One Guinea, to be carried to the account of the Club.

10. The Secretary shall announce to the Club the names of all Visitors.

11. All new Regulations, and all alterations of existing Regulations, shall be proposed at one Meeting, and considered at the next.

12. At the beginning of each season a *Managing Committee* of Three Members shall be appointed to make any necessary arrangements for the Club during the season.

13. At the end of each season a Supervising Committee of Five Members shall be appointed to consider of the interests of the Society during the recess. Three to be a quorum.

14. The Managing Committee propose the Chairman and Deputy-Chairman for the day.

15. At each Meeting any Member has the privilege of proposing as many Questions on Political Economy as he pleases for the consideration of the Club. These must be delivered in writing to the Secretary, subscribed with the name of the proposer.

16. Previous to the adjournment of any Meeting, the Secretary is required to read the newly-proposed Questions, and during the intervals between the Meetings to have all the Questions standing for discussion printed, and distributed to the Members of the Club.

17. The Questions are to be examined at subsequent Meetings in any order, which may seem good to the Club.

18. The Proposer of a Question, if present, opens the Discussion of it.

19. In case at any Meeting the Secretary shall declare there are fewer than three Questions standing for examination at the subsequent Meetings, the Chairman of the day is required to call upon any Members present to contribute each one Question, till the number is made up to six.

20. At the end of each session the Treasurer is required to make out his accounts, and lay the same before the Superintending Committee.

21. When the accounts of the Treasurer have been examined by the Superintending Committee, the Secretary is required to enter them in the books of the Society.

22. All Members of the Club who have been, or shall become, *Cabinet Ministers*, shall become Honorary Members, and their places shall be filled up; no Subscriptions be received from them; but the invitations and Question Papers shall be sent to them.

23. Members of the Club who have been, or shall be, appointed to any permanent situation abroad, shall be considered Supernumerary Members; their places filled up; no Subscriptions received from them; and on their return they shall become Acting Members, and fill the first vacancies that may occur.

24. During the discussion of a Question by the Club, all observations shall be addressed to the Chairman or Deputy-Chairman, whichever may be most distant from the person speaking.

25. The last rule shall be superseded only during the period of tea, the commencement and termination of which shall be declared by the Chairman.

26. The discussion of each Question shall be terminated by the Chairman calling on the Member who opened the Question to reply, after which no Member shall be allowed to continue the discussion.

The following Paragraphs appear in the Original Rules of the Club, adopted at its formation in 1821 :—

The Members of this Society will regard their own mutual instruction, and the diffusion amongst others of the just principles of Political Economy as a real and important obligation.

As the Press is the grand instrument for the diffusion of knowledge or of error, all the Members of this Society will regard it as incumbent upon

E

them to watch carefully the proceedings of the Press, and to ascertain if any doctrines hostile to sound views on Political Economy have been propagated; to contribute whatever may be in their power to refute such erroneous doctrines, and counteract their influence; and to avail themselves of every favourable opportunity for the publication of seasonable truths within the province of this science.

It shall be considered the duty of this Society, individually and collectively, to aid the circulation of all Publications which they deem useful to the science, by making the merits of them known as widely as possible, and to limit the influence of hurtful publications by the same means.

PART IV.

—

In the year 1856—7, the Club reprinted in two Octavo Volumes a series of scarce and valuable Tracts on Economical subjects. For the Tracts selected, and for the editing and superintendence of the two Volumes, the Club were indebted to MR. McCULLOCH.

The contents of the two Volumes were as follows :—

VOL. I.

SELECT TRACTS ON MONEY.

—

CONTENTS.

I. A discourse of Coin and Coinage; the first Invention, Use, Matter, Forms, Proportions and Differences, ancient and modern, with the

Advantages and Disadvantages of the Rise or Fall thereof, in our own or neighbouring Nations; and the Reasons, together with a short account of our Common Law therein. By RICE VAUGHAN, late of Grayes Inn, Esquire. 1675. (120 pp.)

II. A Speech by SIR ROBERT COTTON, Knt. and Bart., before the Lords of his Majesty's most Honourable Privy Council, at the Council Table; being thither called to deliver his opinion touching the alteration of Coin, September 2nd. Anno Regni Regis Caroli I. 1626. (21 pp.)

III. Advice of his Majesty's Council of Trade, concerning the exportation of Gold and Silver in Foreign Coins and Bullion. Concluded 11th December, 1660. (12 pp.)

IV. Sir WILLIAM PETTY, his Quantulumcunque concerning Money. To the LORD MARQUIS of Halyfax, Anno 1682. (14 pp.)

V. A Report containing an Essay for the Amendment of the Silver Coins. 1695. (90 pp.)

VI. Note on the Re-Coinage, 1696—99. (8 pp.)

VII. Representations of SIR ISAAC NEWTON on the subject of Money, 1712—1717. (14 pp.)

VIII. Tables Illustrative of the Successive Changes in the Standard, in the Weight of the Coins, and in the relative Values of Gold and Silver in England, from the Conquest down to 1717. (4 pp.)

IX. Note on Scotch Money with Tables; showing the Successive Changes in the Standard, in the Weight of the Coins, and in the relative Values of Gold and Silver, from 1107 to 1707, when Scotland ceased to have a peculiar Coinage. (4 pp.)

X. Observations on Coin in General, with some Proposals for Regulating the Value of Coin in Ireland. By the Author of the "List of the Absentees of Ireland." 1729. (48 pp.)

XI.   An Essay upon Money and Coins, Part I.,
The Theories of Commerce, Money, and
Exchanges. 1757. (92 pp.)

XII.   An Essay upon Money and Coins, Part II.,
wherein is shewed, that the Established Standard of Money should not be violated or
altered under any pretence whatever. 1758.
(82 pp.)

XIII.   Reflections on Coin in General; on the
Coins of Gold and Silver in Great Britain in
particular; on those Metals as Merchandise,
and also on Paper passing as Money. 1762.
(12 pp.)

XIV.   An Enquiry into the Value of the Ancient
Greek and Roman Money.   By MATTHEW
ROPER, ESQ., F.R.S., from the "Philosophical
Transactions," Vol. LXI. for 1771.   (60 pp.)

XV.   Tables showing the Denominations of the
principal Greek and Roman Coins, and their
Values in Sterling Money.   (10 pp.)

VOL. II.

EARLY TRACTS ON COMMERCE.

CONTENTS.

I. A Discourse of Trade from England unto the East Indies. By T. M., 1621. (48 pp.)

II. The Treasure of Traffike, or a Discourse of Forraigne Trade. By LEWES ROBERTS, 1641. (66 pp.)

III. England's Treasure by Forraign Trade, or the Ballance of our Forraign Trade is the rule of our Treasure. By THOMAS MUN, 1664. (96 pp.)

IV. England's Interest and Improvement. By SAMUEL FORTREY, ESQ., 1673. (40 pp.)

V. England's Great Happiness, or a Dialogue between Content and Complaint. By a real and hearty Lover of his King and Countrey, 1677. (24 pp.)

VI. Britannia Languens, or a Discourse of Trade, 1680. (30 pp.)

VII. Discourses upon Trade, 1691. (36 pp.)

VIII. Considerations on the East India Trade, 1701. (90 pp.)

PART V.

QUESTIONS DISCUSSED,

1860—72.

1860.—*6th December.*

MR. MACLEOD.—To what extent are considerations of Justice and Morality admissible in the discussion of Questions of Political Economy? (12).

1861.—*6th February.*

MR. J. A. HANKEY.—Considering that the extra services and the extra supplies of Commodities required for the purposes of a War are actually provided or consumed during each year of War,

NOTE.—The figures within brackets, *e. g.*, (12) indicate the number of persons (members and visitors) present at the several meetings.

how far, if at all, is it true that a Loan enables
the Community to throw part of the burden of
the War upon posterity ?

(17).

1861.—*7th March.*

MR. NEWMARCH.—Are there any reasons for believing
that a law designed to diminish the prevalence
of Credit in the Country by denying legal
validity to Debts of longer standing than, say
six months, would be economically advantageous ?

(18).

1861.—11*th April.*

MR. MILL.—What is the value of Moral Education
to Economical Improvement ; and conversely,
what are the bearings of Economical Prosperity
on Moral Excellence ?

(22).

1861.—*2nd May.*

MR. LOWE.—Is an uniform Income Tax in accordance with the just principles of Taxation ?
(28).

1861.—*6th June.*

MR. ROGERS.—What is the most convenient definition of the word " Tax " ?
(19).

1861.—*4th July.*

MR. SENIOR.—What is the most convenient definition of Political Economy ?
(18).

1861.—*5th December.*

MR. THRING.—What are the legitimate limitations to be applied, on Economical grounds, to the absolute power of Settling Property ?
(18).

1862.—6th *February.*

Mr. Cowell.—Observation of the Phenomena exhibited in the processes of Production, Distribution, Interchange and Consumption of Wealth having indicated certain laws, or rules, as governing, or naturally attending upon these processes respectively, does observance or disregard of those laws or rules affect the Stability of Nations and Communities according as, in their fiscal and commercial legislation, they observe or violate them ?

(24).

1862.—6th *March.*

Mr. Rogers.—What are the grounds on which the Legislature awards an exclusive privilege of Professional Practice in certain callings ; and is such a privilege advantageous to the public, and desirable for the Practitioner ?

(22).

1862.—*3rd April.*

MR. FAWCETT.—Can the present Poll Tax, which is imposed upon Chinese Immigrants into Australia, be defended on Economic grounds ? (21).

1862.—*29th April.*

MR. NEWMARCH.—In the present state of Railway enterprise in this Country, how far is it true that the public convenience and profit may be best advanced by promoting the Amalgamation of Lines, with a view to a regulated Monopoly, rather than by encouraging competition in the ordinary sense ? (16).

1862.—*5th June.*

MR. THORNTON.—Can any Income Tax, and, *a fortiori*, an uniform Income Tax, be otherwise than at variance with the just principles of Taxation ? (25).

1862.—10*th July.*

MR. MERIVALE.—Does Political Economy afford any tests for ascertaining at what period the maintenance by the Mother Country of dominion over a Colony ceases to be profitable? (By Colony is meant, for the purpose of this question, one founded by the Mother Country and peopled wholly or in great part by Emigration from it.)

(20).

1862.—4*th December.*

MR. NEWMARCH.—What kind of Taxes are best adapted to a British Colony in the situation of Canada at this time?

(16)

1863.—6*th February.*

SIR STAFFORD NORTHCOTE.—Would England gain more in material resources by the adoption of

measures for the protection of private Property from Capture at Sea, in time of War, than she would lose by the abandonment of the right of injuring her enemy by the seizure of such Property ?

(26)

1863.—*6th March.*

SIR ROWLAND HILL.—Is it expedient that the Cab Fares in London and elsewhere should be fixed by Law ?

(22)

1863.—*27th March.*

MR. MILL.—What is the best definition of Productive and Unproductive Labour, and of Productive and Unproductive Consumption ?

(16)

1863.—1st *May*.

Mr. FAWCETT.—To what extent is the principle of Co-operative Trade Societies among the Working Classes economically sound ?

(23)

1863.—5th *June*.

Mr. CLIFFE LESLIE.—Has the discovery of New Gold Mines made any change in the conditions of International Trade ?

(20)

1863.—3rd *July*.

Mr. MILL.—Is the word Capital most properly used to designate certain kinds of wealth, namely, food, implements and materials ; or should it rather be applied to all wealth, of whatever kind, which is, or is intended by its owner to be, applied to the purpose of Re-production ?

(22)

1863.—*4th December.*

Mr. Merivale.—When a Loan is to bo raised for warlike or other unproductive expenditure, is it more advantageous (on general principles) to borrow of Countrymen or of Foreigners ?
(18).

1864.—*5th February.*

Mr. Thomson Hankey.—To what extent is the power of a Country to make or carry on War destroyed or diminished by what are called Financial Difficulties ?
(18).

1864.—*4th March.*

Mr. Chadwick.—Is the ownership of Land, with the intent to its Culture by the Labour of the Owner, and the Members of his Family, economically expedient ?
(20).

1864.—*8th April.*

Mr. Rogers.—What are the elements which should be reckoned in any numerical calculation of National Wealth?
(19).

1864.—*6th May.*

Mr. Cowell.—As Government exists to protect Property and Person, it is just that each man should contribute towards maintaining Government in proportion to the total value of the property possessed *by* him, and protected *for* him, and it is unjust that any man should contribute in any other proportion. An uniform Percentage Tax on the value of each man's protected property being perfectly equitable, is there any other equally equitable Tax, less likely to interfere injuriously with the natural processes of the Production, Distribution, Interchange, and Consumption of Wealth than this?
(18).

1864.—*3rd June.*

MR. MERIVALE.—The obligations of a State having been contracted in a Silver Currency, is there any foundation for the opinion that there is a breach of faith committed towards the holders by substituting or adding Gold as a standard ? (22).

1864.—*1st July.*

MR. THORNTON.—What would be the effect on Literary Produce and Literary Producers of a total abolition of Copyright ? (23).

1864.—*2nd December.*

MR. FITZJAMES STEPHEN.—Upon what principles of Political Economy ought the law of Parochial Settlement to be founded ? (18).

1865.— *3rd February.*

Mr. Chadwick.—What are the leading principles of Political Economy applicable in this Country to the initiation, construction, and working of Railways for public use ?
(26).

1865.—*3rd March.*

Mr. Bagehot.—Are there any circumstances which should induce us to think that the average Rate of Interest in this Country has a tendency to rise as compared with the Rate (say) ten years back ?
(22).

1865.—*7th April.*

Mr. Merivale.—Is it expedient, in an economical point of view, that breaches of engagement (for instance between Vendor and Purchaser, Debtor

and Creditor, Trustee and Cestuique Trust, Employer and Servant, or Workman) should be subject to punishment, as offences against Criminal Law ; and if it is, can any practicable limitation of the principle be laid down ? (16).

1865.—*5th May.*

REV. J. E. T. ROGERS.—Are there any circumstances in the history of a community which will justify Protection on Economical grounds ? (20).

1865.—*2nd June.*

MR. CAIRNES.—What is the true relation of Money to the rate of Interest ? (21.)

1865.—7th *July.*

MR. MILL.—Does the high rate of Interest in America and in new Colonies, indicate a corresponding high rate of Profits? and if so, what are the causes of that high rate?
(24).

1865.—1st *December.*

REV. J. E. T. ROGERS.—Is it possible to define *a priori* the just limits between *laissez faire* and defensible interference by a Legislature with the industry or pursuits of its subjects?
(18).

1866.—2nd *February.*

MR. BAGEHOT.—Is it, or is it not desirable to append an Expansive Clause to the Act of 1844, permitting, in cases of internal panic, the Chancellor of the Exchequer and the First Lord of

the Treasury, on the application of the Bank of England, to augment the Issue of Bank Notes upon Securities beyond the limit now prescribed ?

(31).

1866.—*2nd March.*

Mr. FAWCETT.—Is it not incorrect to affirm that Poor Rates are solely a charge on Land, inasmuch as they are often really paid by the occupiers of Houses, and by the consumers of Commodities ?

(12).

1866.—*30th April.*

Mr. CLIFFE LESLIE.—On Economical principles, ought the relation of Landlord and Tenant to be left to private interest, the State interfering only to secure the performance of the Contract ?

(20).

1866.—*4th May.*

Mr. Merivale.—Under what circumstances, independent of political emergencies, is it desirable to negotiate with a Foreign State in order to effect a Commercial Treaty?

(22).

1866.—*1st June.*

Mr. Waley.—A Country is burdened with a heavy perpetual debt, the Interest of which forms from a third to a half of its ordinary expenditure. It is probable that its means for producing Wealth are likely to undergo serious diminution; such diminution, however, not to commence for a long period, say for a Century. Is it, or is it not desirable that the Legislature of that Country, in fixing its annual Taxation, should take into account this probability?

(22).

1866.—*6th July.*

MR. BAGEHOT.—Is it better to intrust the principal Custody of the Bullion Reserve against Banking liabilities to a single Bank, or to distribute it between several Banks
(27).

1866.—*7th December.*

MR. THORNTON.—What is the meaning of Supply, and what of Demand? Is it correct to say that supply and demand determine price? If not, in what manner is it that supply and demand affect price?
(18).

1867.—*1st February.*

MR. NEWMARCH.—Is there reason to believe that it has become practicable in this Country to Establish on a large scale, plans under which persons

H

employed may be remunerated, wholly or partly, by participation in the profit and loss results of the businesses carried on by their employers? (25).

1867.—1*st March.*

MR. MERIVALE.—What measures would it be advisable for the Government of India to take, in accordance as far as possible with sound Economical Policy, to prevent the occurrence of Famines extending over considerable districts of Country, or to mitigate their effects. (21).

1867.—5*th April.*

MR. BAGEHOT.—In what form, if any, could the principles of so-called "Tenant Right" be applied in Ireland? (24). -

1867.—*3rd May.*

Mr. WALEY.—In what manner, and under what conditions, if any, can the British Government properly afford assistance to Railway Companies, with a view to their relief from temporary or accidental embarrassment ?
(21).

1867.—*7th June.*

Mr. LESLIE.—What are the comparative advantages or disadvantages of the different systems in use in great States for raising and recruiting an Army, economically considered, in reference both to Military efficiency and to Cost ?
(23).

1867.—*5th July.*

Mr. HARE.—What Legislation, if any, either modifying the general laws of immoveable property, or conferring special facilities, financial or

otherwise, would be desirable, in order to pro-
mote the erection of adequate Dwellings for the
Working Classes, and the disposal of such
dwellings among them when erected ?
(22).

1867.—6th *December.*

MR. NEWMARCH.—What are the reasons, if any,
which justify those clauses of the present
Succession Duty Acts in this country which
limit the Tax, in the case of Real Estate, to
the value of the life interest only of the Suc-
cessor ?
(17).

1868.—7th *February.*

MR. MERIVALE.—Is it, or is it not, desirable to give
any legislative privileges or facilities to Friendly
Societies, which are not conceded to Trades
Unions?
(21).

1868.—*6th March.*

MR. NEWMARCH.—Has the compulsory division in France of Landed Property among the descendants of deceased owners, been Economically beneficial to that Country or the reverse ? (24).

1868.—*3rd April.*

LORD DUFFERIN.—Has the Emigration of late years from Ireland been disadvantageous, or the reverse, to that Country ? (27).

1868.—*1st May.*

Mr. WATKIN.—What is the true policy to be pursued in this Country regarding the authorisation of Railways—to sanction, as at present, any Railway proposed, or only to authorise such Lines as will produce an adequate Dividend ? (20).

1868.—*5th June.*

MR. CHADWICK.—What Economical grounds are there for charging upon Personal Property any portion of the expense of Local administration now charged upon Real Property?
(12).

1868.—*3rd July.*

MR. BAGEHOT.—Are the principles upon which the Banking Department of the Bank of England should be managed, identical with those which should regulate any other large London Bank?
(19).

1868.—*4th December.*

MR. NEWMARCH.—Are there any special merits or defects in the plan adopted by the United States for providing the interest, and reducing the principal of the National Debt?
(11).

1869.—*5th February.*

MR. BAGEHOT.—Ought a Government to impose a Seigniorage on Coins which are legal tender for an unlimited amount, and if it ought, how much should such Seigniorage be ?

(22).

1869.—*5th March.*

MR. GREG.—Is it true, upon economic principles, that the Commercial relation between Employers and Labourers for hire is necessarily one of antagonism ?

(15).

1869.—*2nd April.*

LORD FREDERICK CAVENDISH.—Is the system of Local Taxation in this country adequate to meet the demands upon it, and if not, in what manner can it be supplemented ?

(19).

1869.—*2nd May*.

MR. CHADWICK.—What Economical advantages are derivable from the Elementary Education and the Physical Training of the Population, to justify a compulsory system and payment for it by Rates and Taxes.
(18).

1869.—*4th June*.

MR. WALEY.—Is the rule of English Law by which contracts in restraint of Trade are prohibited in accordance with sound Economical Policy ?
(28).

1869.—*2nd July*.

MR. LESLIE —Is the doctrine of the equality of the Rate of Profits well founded ?
(21).

1869.—*3rd December.*

PROFESSOR ROGERS.—Does the theory of the different fertility of soils account for the origin and increase of Rent, and if not, how is the phenomenon of Rent to be explained ?
(18).

1870.—*4th February.*

MR. BAGEHOT.—In what manner is the Ulster Tenant Right to be reconciled with the ordinary doctrines of Political Economy respecting Rent, and to what extent does it serve as a guide for future legislation as to Irish Land ?
(22).

1870.—*4th March.*

MR. TORRENS.—To what extent has it been found necessary in the Australian Colonies to modify during recent years the Wakefield principle in its application to the disposal of Waste Lands ?
(14).

1870.—*1st April.*

MR. CAIRNES.—Assuming that the State undertake to settle by legislation the relation of Landlord and Tenant, can any criterion be suggested for determining Agricultural Rent in conformity with the moral basis of property, and consistently with public policy?
(21).

1870.—*6th May.*

MR. MERIVALE.—What are the economical advantages or disadvantages arising to this Country from the possession of India?
(23).

1870.—*3rd June.*

MR. NEWMARCH.—To what extent can the Government of this Country interfere with advantage with the business of Life Insurance Offices, with the view of preventing mismanagement and insolvency.
(18).

1870.—1st *July.*

Mr. Waley.—Is it to be expected that material Economical advantages would result from restraining the latitude of Settlement and Entail of Land allowed by the Law of England ?
(25).

1870.—2nd *December.*

Mr. Hare.—What are the valid objections, if any, to the adoption, under present circumstances, of an uniform Poor Law Rating over the whole of the Metropolis ?
(17).

1871.—3rd *February.*

Sir Charles W. Dilke.—Would the institution of Free Schools have a tendency to pauperize the parents of the children who might be taught in them ?
(18).

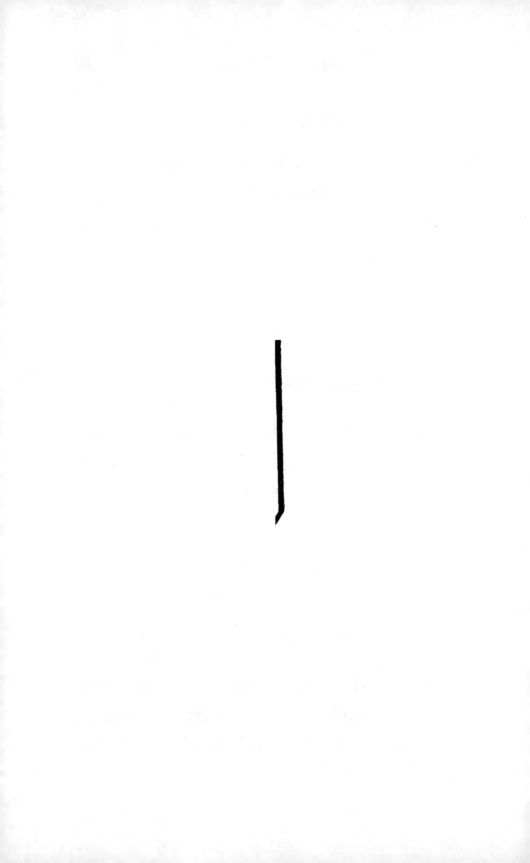

1871.—*3rd March.*

MR. CHADWICK.—Was Adam Smith correct in his view that Standing Armies are the most economical form of Military force ?
(25).

1871.—*31st March.*

MR. COURTNEY.—Is the limitation correct which is involved in the title of the Theory of International Trade ?
(23).

1871.—*5th May.*

MR. NEWMARCH.—How far is it true that after the cessation of such a war as recently prevailed between France and Germany, there is a tendency in the belligerent Countries to rapid recovery from the loss of Wealth occasioned by the conflict ?
(18).

1871.—*2nd June.*

MR. FARRER.—Assuming that there are Industrial Undertakings which competition cannot regulate, what is their character, and the best mode of dealing with them ?
(24).

1871.—*7th July.*

MR. BAGEHOT.—Upon what principles, if any, can an Arbitrator between Masters and Men, during a Strike, decide in favour of one or other ?
(21).

1871.—*1st December.*

MR. NEWMARCH.—How far is it true that the French Commercial Treaty of 1860, and subsequent Treaties on the same basis, are in accordance with sound Economical principles ?
(15).

1872.—*2nd February.*

Mr. Bagehot.—It has been proposed to appropriate to the use of the State the increment of the rent of lands consequent on the development of Society. In such a Country as England is it practicable or desirable to act on this proposal ?

(23).

1872.—*1st March.*

Mr. Hare.—May not lands be permitted with advantage to be held for Public or Charitable uses, supposing the management of such lands were vested in local and responsible Government Officers, instructed to regard the general welfare, as well as the benefit of the Institutions receiving the Income ?

(18).

1872.—*5th April.*

MR. CHADWICK.—What is likely to be the effect of the Nine hours movement, if made general, on the productive power of this Country ? (16).

1872.—*3rd May.*

MR. WALEY.—Is it the fact that the Wage Fund Theory, or Doctrine that wages depend on the proportion of Capital to Population, has been displaced by recent Economical investigations ? (14).

1872.—*7th June.*

SIR LOUIS MALLET.—Is it desirable on Economic grounds to maintain the existing proportion between direct and indirect Taxation in this Country ? (25).

1872.—*5th July.*

MR. GREG.—Is open competition the universal and unmixed economic good it is usually represented to be ?

(20).

PART VI.

QUESTIONS ON THE MEETING PAPER AT THE CLOSE OF THE SESSION, 1871—2.

1. In what manner, as far as can be ascertained or seems probable, have the New Gold Mines affected Prices ?

MR. LESLIE.

2. What are the circumstances, if any, which in this Country would justify the State or Municipal Authorities in providing or contributing to the cost of Improved Dwellings for the Poorer Classes ?

MR. NEWMARCH.

3. When the State, for reasons of Economy or improved administration, has to dismiss persons in its employment, what are the principles which should determine the amount and kind of pecuniary compensation to be awarded ?

MR. WALEY.

4. Is the reasoning sound which discriminates between Capital and Income in discussing the principles of Direct Taxation ?

MR. COURTNEY.

K

5. On Economical grounds, what are the reasons, if any, for the retention of Canada by this country ?

MR. NEWMARCH.

6. Are there any circumstances which may warrant the adoption by nations of Protective measures directed against certain results of " Free Trade in Labour ? "

SIR CHARLES DILKE.

7. In what form, if at all, can the principle of a Sinking Fund be applied to the Public Debt of this Country ?

MR. NEWMARCH.

8. What are the principles which should govern the action of the State, in dealing with Waste Lands ?

SIR CHARLES DILKE.

9. In the formation of Customs' Unions, what kinds of duties should be imposed, and how should the revenue resulting from them be distributed ?

MR. COURTNEY.

10. Is the objection to Mr. Malthus's theory of Population, grounded on the supposed physiological law that fecundity is in proportion to poverty, a valid objection ?

MR. GREG.

K 2

11. Is there any justification on Economic grounds for the present Law of Distraint for Rent in England, and of Hypothec in Scotland, under which the landlord obtains practically a preference over other creditors ?

MR. NEWMARCH.

12. Political Economy being the Science which treats of National Wealth, in what sense should the word Wealth be understood, when used in politico-economical discussions ?

MR. THORNTON.

SUGGESTED QUESTIONS.

13. To what extent, if any, would Farmers be benefited by the Repeal of the Malt Tax ?

14. Can the Government of this Country undertake with advantage the control of Friendly Societies for the Working Classes ?

15. How far is the proposal to raise part of the Poor Law Expenditure of this country by an addition to the Income Tax, in accordance with sound economic policy ?

16. Is there any sufficient reason for exempting from the operation of a Tax on Income the revenues of Charitable Institutions ?

17. In what manner can Bankrupt Railways be best dealt with, so as to secure the interests of the Creditors and the Public ?

18. What modifications, if any, are required in the Taxation of the United Kingdom, so as to render it more productive of revenue and more equitable to the various classes of contributors ?

19. What are the considerations, if any, which should induce a Country to discourage or prevent the Exportation of Commodities in the production of which it possesses pre-eminent or exclusive advantages ?

20. What is the most convenient definition of the word "Demand ?"

21. Do Profits depend in any degree, and, if in any, how far, on the fact of Commodities being usually sold or exchanged for others before being consumed ?

22. To what extent, if any, have the Poorer Classes of this Country partaken of the large increase of the last hundred years in Wealth, and its attendant conveniences ?

23. What is the nature of the process by which the influx of the New Gold from California and Australia has added and is adding to the Real Wealth of the World ?

24. How far ought the experience acquired since the time of Malthus to modify our views respecting the truth of the principles laid down by him on the subject of Population, or their importance in their bearing on Social and Political Questions ?

25. What are the causes which prevent the Poorest Classes in this Country from enjoying a larger Share in the advantages of our increasing Wealth and the progress of Improvement ?

26. To what extent is an increase in the price of Stock Exchange Securities an increase in Public Wealth ?

27. What is the most convenient definition of the term "Raw Materials ?"

28. Are there any sound reasons for considering the Price of Labour to imply any economical conditions essentially different from those implied by the Price of Commodities ?

29. For purposes of Taxation, what is the most scientific and practical definition of the word "Income ?"

PART VII.

INDEX TO QUESTIONS DISCUSSED, 1860—72.

UNWIN BROTHERS, PRINTERS, LONDON AND CHILWORTH.

CPSIA information can be obtained
at www.ICGtesting.com
Printed in the USA
BVHW08s0824170918
527707BV00023B/796/P